Keep Him Coming Home with Love

Be Intentional about Strengthening Your Bond

Shenitha Finesse Anniece Burton

S.H.E. PUBLISHING, LLC

© Copyright 2020 by S.H.E. Publishing, LLC.

All rights reserved. This book or any portion thereof may not be reproduced or used in any manner whatsoever without the express written permission of the publisher except for the use of brief quotations in a book review.

ISBNs
Paperback: 978-1-7350327-0-2
Ebook: 978-1-7350327-1-9
Hard cover: 978-1-7350327-2-6
Special Edition Paperback: 978-1-7350327-3-3

This book is dedicated to my husband of twenty years; our parents, who made sure we never witnessed the obstacles they faced; my sister-in-law who has been a great role model to my daughters; and my four amazing daughters, who will one day understand the meaning of love in a different context. This book is also dedicated to the men and women who are trying to build better relationships and contribute valuable insights to others in their lives, young and old. Everybody has a unique story to tell.

Contents

Introduction vii

Chapter One   The Journey of *L*: Learning and
Loving Each Other 1
Moment One: Driver's Education Class 2
Moment Two: Learning Our Strengths and
    Making the Relationship Work 5

Chapter Two   The Journey of *O*: Overcoming Obstacles 7
Moment Three: Reliving the Past 9
Moment Four: Building a Brighter Future 13

Chapter Three   The Journey of *V*: Valuing Family Traditions 17
Moment Five: Father's Day Picnics 18
Moment Six: Gathering Together on
    Holidays and Birthdays 19

Chapter Four   The Journey of *E*: Enlarging the Family Vision .. 23
Moment Seven: The Burton Billionaires 24
Moment Eight: Showtime Exclusive Wheels 27

Parting Thoughts 29
Coming Soon! Keep Him Coming Home with Love 33
Acknowledgments 35
About the Author 37

Introduction

Congratulations! You have begun the journey of reading and/or listening to this book and have entered the realm of receiving valuable ideas that you can apply to your personal life, or you can gift this book to someone who's just beginning the journey to build a relationship. *Keep Him Coming Home with Love* is a four-book series that touches on being intentional about creating a bond not only with your mate but also with your entire family and your friends. It's okay to be intentional in your relationships. This particular book will intentionally focus on Love:

Learning and loving each other
Overcoming obstacles
Valuing family traditions
Enlarging the family vision

When I think of the past, I remember how a traditional relationship between a man and a woman used to be: husbands wore the pants and were the breadwinners, while wives took care of the home, nurtured the family, and assisted the husband. Times have surely changed. As we try to compete with social media and all of the instances of negativity, it is getting harder and harder to build strong relationships. So in addition to attending church and visiting counselors, reading this book offers another way for couples to share with each other and work together to build a stronger bond within their relationship. In this book I will share some of my most private moments. These are the ingredients that explain why I am still a married woman today;

however, as with any recipe, you have to adjust the ingredients to your taste. A relationship is no different.

Your life can change in the blink of an eye if you don't prepare for a possible 911 situation. In continuing to prepare for challenging moments in my life, I have acquired a PhD in knowing how to stay married for twenty years. Sharing my world with the man of my dreams for twenty-six years has allowed me to make mistakes, gain wisdom from my experiences, and learn from others. My Father God, who protects me and my family, has poured different ideas into me. My cup runneth over. I truly believe that everything happens for a reason and that our experiences are the preparation for what's to come. I have spent countless days and nights coming up with ideas to create stronger marriages. With that said, I have been intentional and strategic about when, what, and how I move within my relationship, especially in the relationship I have with my man.

I am confident that the sooner you delve into *Keep Him Coming Home with Love*, the sooner you will be able to relate to, use, and/or share the ideas in this book to help build your relationship with your man or significant others in your life. *Keep Him Coming Home with Love*.

CHAPTER ONE

The Journey of L: Learning and Loving Each Other

*We should really love each other
in peace and harmony.*
—Bob Marley

Had I only known as a young adult what I know now, my relationships would have gone much smoother with a number of people in my life. Had I known my individual strengths, I would have known how to wield them from the balcony, and had I known my weaknesses, I would have known how to manage them from the basement.

Building relationships can be a challenge, but it becomes easier when you know yourself better. You become more mature, wiser, and you begin to understand what you lead with (i.e., executing, influencing, relationship building, or strategic thinking – four domains from the book *StrengthFinders 2.0* by Tom Rath), which all contribute to the decisions you make in life. The nugget for today is to embark on the journey of learning and knowing who you are and to seek to learn how people around you operate as well. My journey of learning how to build, and then building, a solid relationship with my husband of twenty years started in a driver's education class. I had no clue at that moment that he would be the man I would marry and with whom I would share four beautiful daughters. Jermaine was to become the man who would contribute to my roller coaster ride of love.

Moment One: Driver's Education Class

> *Tell me and I forget. Teach me and I remember. Involve me and I learn.*
> —Benjamin Franklin

As I sat in a chair in my driver's education class during my sophomore year at Marie Sklowdowska Curie High School, a question was posed to the students by the teacher. A guy sitting four seats to my right raised his hand and began to speak. He was a fine, light-skinned young man who had luscious lips similar to LL Cool J's lips and a smile that made me melt like butter sizzles in a hot skillet. He answered a question to which I did not know the answer, and to my surprise he didn't know the answer either. He was confident in his response, and the entire class chuckled, including me, when his answer was incorrect. Not only was he fine, but he also knew how to make everyone in the room laugh with his wrong answers. Now that's impressive. That is the moment that plays out in my mind the most often, and it is a day I will never forget.

Who doesn't like a man who makes them laugh? My husband and his friend Kevin attended the driver's education class at my high school because their school didn't offer the class. My husband has a very charming personality, and many students were checking him out. I needed to stand out from the crowd to secure the merchandise—the young man who would one day be my husband. So what did I do? I took his driver's education book and put it down my shirt. I can see you shaking your head and thinking, "What a mischievous young lady you were." I know I was, but I just had to do something. I then told him to come and get it. I know that wasn't very ladylike, but it sure did intrigue him, and it turned his attention my way.

I wasn't really going to allow this attractive and desirable brother to reach down my shirt, but that's the fantasy that presented itself to me. It had him thinking, "What would it be like?" Several of his senses would be involved if he took the bait that I was dangling in front of him: the sight of my lace undergarments as he retrieved his book from underneath my shirt, the pleasant scent of the fragrance I was wearing, the feel of my soft, tender skin, and the sound of a sweet love song playing in our minds. I truly wasn't thinking of the depth of this situation at that time. It's just something that frequently plays out in my mind because at that moment I truly wasn't trying to be intentional; I was just trying to have some fun.

After our driver's education class ended, I did not see him again until a year later. I was wearing a black skirt and a cute white blouse, and I was ready to enjoy the party of the year—homecoming! Who doesn't like homecoming? You get to dress up, hang out with all your friends, take lots of pictures, and have a good time meeting new people who come to your school for the event. As I was walking with my friends after getting our pictures taken, who did I run into? You guessed it. It was the gorgeous brother from driver's education class. All I remember is his vibrant smile and the red Nike shirt he was wearing. We spoke, and I was surprised that he actually remembered me. And you know how it goes when you don't want to seem too thirsty, so you have to gracefully exit the conversation to portray yourself as having other pressing matters to attend to. Later during the evening, a few guys began to ask me to dance, but I said no each time. I wanted you-know-who to ask me to dance. I could see him from the corner of my eye, watching as I turned down guy after guy. Was he ever going to ask me to dance? I finally found myself in his arms dancing to one of my favorite songs. After that delightful night, I still didn't call that handsome and personable brother. What was wrong with me?

A month or so later, as I walked through the hallway of my high school, Eric, a friend of mine who is also a friend of my now husband of twenty years, walked up to me and said, "Call my boy," as he handed me my future husband's phone number. Eric was prepared to lay it on thick so that I would agree to call his homie. This felt like it could result in strike three for me, so I had to call him. It took me about two to three days to call him, and when I did, we talked hour after hour all night long. The rest would be history. Our story turned into "the Jermaine and Finesse Saga."

Moment Two: Learning Our Strengths and Making the Relationship Work

> *The better you know yourself, the better your relationship with the rest of the world.*
> —Toni Collette

As my husband and I became closer and the years passed by, we were presented with challenges. One of our challenges was building a family. I became pregnant at the age of twenty and delivered my first baby girl at age twenty-one. I didn't have the luxury of enjoying an alcoholic beverage for my twenty-first birthday. I had to drink sparkling water. Although I was in a relationship with the love of my life, and we'd been in a committed relationship for four years, I really didn't know who he was. As a matter of fact, I still didn't fully understand who I was, nor did I know my purpose in life at that point. I sometimes ask myself, can you ever really know a person? Is this person living a double life? One thing I did learn from this relationship is that one needs water to survive, and he was and is my sparkling water.

The challenge of building a family together forced my husband and me to begin to get to know each other on another level. But getting to know each other is more than just learning what each other's favorite color, or favorite food. Getting to know each other became more about how we communicate, what we lead with, and our overall mindset. It was about how we wanted to be celebrated and whether or not we both possess what we need to succeed in this relationship. I'm talking about the kinds of skills, qualities, and characteristics that an employer would ask about in an interview of their prospective hire. In order to strengthen my relationship with my husband, I had to dig deep into the depths of who I am and who he is.

I've worked for the federal courts for twenty-one years, and through my job, I was introduced to a strengths' assessment in the book *StrengthsFinder 2.0*, by Tom Rath. The book helps to identify areas in which one has the greatest potential to build his or her strengths. Each book that is purchased includes a website address and a special code that allows the purchaser to access an assessment that measures recurring patterns of behaviors, feelings, and thoughts. If you answer the questions honestly, when the results are revealed, you will begin to see how you operate, what you lead with, and will have a name for how you have been operating in your life. You will even be able to identify how you have been perceived by others. The assessment generates a report that includes suggestions for how to exercise your strengths. This is a very accurate and resourceful assessment.

Jermaine and I each took the assessment separately, and it has been very beneficial to us as a couple. I encourage you, your significant other, friends, and family to take the assessment or a similar assessment that allows you to learn more about yourself and your strengths. It is true, as Toni Collette reminded us at the beginning of this chapter, that when you know yourself, the better your relationships are with the people in your world. Jermaine and I continue to learn more and more about ourselves daily. We still have passionate conversations, but we are able to communicate to each other how we operate to avoid misunderstandings in the future. It is also important to respect and understand the differences in each other, which will ultimately lead to building a stronger bond.

CHAPTER TWO

The Journey of O: Overcoming Obstacles

If a man wants you, nothing can keep him away. If he doesn't want you, nothing can make him stay.
—Oprah Winfrey

I would say the first five to ten years of my marriage included several moments of overcoming obstacles. In most relationships, this statement tends to be true for different reasons. Overcoming obstacles in my relationship primarily involved Jermaine and me getting to know each other. Every human being is different. The point at which I entered into a relationship with him became a factor in the challenge because I was very young. It didn't help the situation that we had a baby within the beginning stages of our relationship, so we were not really able to enjoy each other as adults. Infidelity would become an obstacle as well.

Other obstacles can include bringing along children from a previous relationship, not wanting to have children, and not wanting more children when the other spouse does want them. In addition to children, other obstacles might include the marriage being your second or third, financial difficulties, and your spouse thinking your marriage should be like marriages are portrayed on television. I think you would agree that the list can go on and on, depending on your individual circumstances. These are obstacles that our parents and grandparents have faced, but for some reason previous generations have not always shared obstacles they have faced with us when we begin to go through adulthood ourselves. When we get hit with a challenge in the relationship, we tend to believe we are the only person who is facing it, when all along our neighbors across the street or our parents could be facing the same challenge at the same moment. I'd say that sharing those moments with our children when they reach the appropriate age, as well as sharing with friends and family whom we trust, can be beneficial, and it also provides a counseling session that is needed in every relationship.

Getting back to Jermaine and me, we met each other at the age of fifteen. We had a beautiful baby girl whom we named Jada Alexis, and we moved in together upon Jada's arrival even though we'd never shared the responsibility of paying bills and building a family together. We had not gone through marriage counseling before we got married, nor were we a couple who prayed together, which I highly recommend all couples do. The benefits of counseling, whether through a church, an agency, or via this book, are that it allows you to begin to better identify the obstacles with which you're presented, and it can also give you a strategy for how to be intentional and strategic in how you deal with those obstacles within your relationship.

Being strategic about how you handle obstacles can include referring to Chapter One, "Moment Two: Learning Our Strengths and Making the Relationship Work," section of this book along with the *Keep Him Coming Home with Love* journal. Writing down those first-moment memories as well as the obstacles you foresee getting in the way of your relationship is the key to being successful in your relationship. Also, my next book, *The Warmth of Your Home Determines the Temperature of Your Relationship*, will provide you with more details regarding how to go about identifying and being strategic about your successful plan of action. The goal is to plan your work and work your plan!

In the next two moments, you will begin to see how the identified obstacle of reliving the past could throw a monkey wrench into your relationship, and you will learn how you can prepare to be strategic in building a brighter future by incorporating all of the details you wrote about your first memories of your relationship and the obstacles I call "911."

Moment Three: Reliving the Past

> *A man can love you from the bottom of*
> *his heart, and still find room at the top for*
> *somebody he claimed was nobody.*
> —Kiki Strack

I remember the scene like it was yesterday. I was sitting comfortably on my plush bed, watching him walk back and forth between the closet and the bed as he packed his bags. He seemed to be struggling to find the words to say, the words I'd been expecting him to say to me for days. But instead of hearing him say, "I'm sorry," the words I heard next would break my heart forever: "It's not you; it's me." What type of nonsense is that to say? What does it even mean? At this point in our relationship, we now had two beautiful daughters. We'd been married for at least five years, and I had been dealing with several challenging moments during that time. When Jermaine began packing his bags to leave me and the girls and move out of the house because we'd had a passionate conversation, I began to think of the promise we had made to each other at the altar. Not only was I hurt, but I was also enraged. We promised to be together for better or for worse, in sickness and in health, and all of that other good stuff. As wives, it is our sworn duty and responsibility to fight for our marriage. Whether you are a celebrity or an ordinary person like me, it is not considered foolish to fight for your love and your marriage. You don't have to become another divorce statistic. However, both people have to be willing to save the marriage, and it may be that each of you is willing at different moments within the marriage-saving challenge.

There was a moment in my marriage where my husband and I separated, and he indeed moved out of our home. As a matter of fact, I actually accompanied him to buy his new home. At that moment, we agreed that I needed to be comfortable with where our children would lay their heads when they were with him. The goal was for us to try to figure out where we each stood in our relationship. We thought we needed space to regroup to focus on moving toward a brighter future, and if we could not move from reliving the past of our mistakes, we'd need to make the decision to go our separate ways legally. I even drafted a separation agreement. One thing about separation is that it brings forth more obstacles, and the obstacle we both had to face was infidelity.

Keep Him Coming Home with Love

A relationship is not a test, so why cheat?
—Author unknown

Learning about my husband's infidelity is a moment I don't ever want to revisit. If you have ever been through infidelity in your relationship, you remember where you were, who you were with, and how you felt when you learned about it. Unlike how the movies sometimes portray spouses catching their partner in the act, I never walked in on my husband when he was cheating. During that stage, I would have a gut feeling, and/or maybe I would see an inappropriate text message or direct message come through on his phone. When you have those gut-wrenching feelings that your partner is not being fully honest, more often than not you are accurate. If you have to hire a detective from the television show *Cheaters*, nine times out of ten, the detective will find that your spouse is cheating or doing something inappropriate with someone else. Because that moment for me has come and gone, it's something that I don't relive or get angry about anymore.

One of the reasons why my husband and I survived this moment is because we both were willing to put forth the effort to save our marriage. When I no longer wanted to be married to Jermaine, and I made the mistake of cheating, he fought for our marriage, and when he no longer wanted to be married to me, I fought for our marriage. We were willing to work on our marriage, but it was at different moments within that challenging time. Again, it's okay to fight to keep the man or woman of your dreams. I knew my man's potential, and he recognized my potential too. During the actual moment of infidelity, I didn't think our marriage would survive, but now that I reflect back on our mistakes and our growth, I can see that sharing my vision of a successful marriage was instilled in both of us, and we were not going to throw away everything we'd worked so hard for. We knew that if we continued to relive the moments of infidelity, it would inevitably lead to that deadly word: divorce. Divorce is definitely the result of reliving the past and not being able to let go of those bitter feelings. It is important to identify how you got to this point, so you don't divorce and then realize too late that you've made the biggest mistake of your life.

I've heard family, friends and even some of my co-workers say that they've never experienced infidelity in a relationship. This is probably true, just like it's true that some parents withhold information from their children regarding situations like infidelity. This book is dedicated to my daughters because I want them to understand that relationships do not always look like those, they see on the Disney channel. Their parents are human, and humans make mistakes. I am hopeful that they won't make the same mistakes their father and I made—one of those mistakes being to continue reliving the past.

Being able to discuss something that occurred in the past and not get angry all over again is a sign of growth. My husband and I have gotten to a place where we are still growing in this area of our lives, and we have made great strides. We are mature enough to know that at the time we made these mistakes, we were young and foolish. Another point I'd like to mention is that as women, we have to be respectful to each other. An obstacle that another woman has faced can turn around and become one that we may have to face. We are women who have mothers, daughters, nieces, aunties, and friends. Each individual girl and woman means something to someone. We're all somebody, and we all have feelings.

During the moment of overcoming obstacles in our relationship, my husband and I were too immature to realize how sacred marriage is and how important it is to live in the present and look forward to our future together. If you are not able to talk about the obstacles of your past or the mistakes you made, you have not healed from what took place in those moments, and it will be hard for you to move forward. What helped me to heal was asking myself the following questions: 1) Are we in this relationship to build together, or are we wasting our time? 2) In what ways has God blessed us? 3) Can recalling the good memories of our past help us to move forward? 4) Is divorce an option we want to consider?

Moment Four: Building a Brighter Future

> *A strong relationship starts with two people who are ready to sacrifice anything for each other.*
> —AUTHOR UNKNOWN

My husband and I renewed our marriage vows around our fifteenth wedding anniversary. It was one of the most beautiful events I've ever planned and attended. The ceremony was held outside on a private terrace. The red bricks on the walkway reminded me of the streets of Old San Juan, Puerto Rico. The cocktail hour was held in an art gallery, and our *Game of Thrones* blanket with our picture on it was displayed on the wall as a masterpiece. The piano in the art gallery added the perfect touch as it would be played during our first dance. The reception was held in a banquet room with burgundy uplights reflecting on the chandeliers. Rectangular and oval tables were adorned with flowers and lit candelabras. We had an amazing vow renewal ceremony and celebration. It was one of the milestones in our lives that contributed to helping us build a brighter future together.

The officiant of our wedding renewal ceremony was the pastor who'd married us fifteen years prior. As Pastor Sylvester Johnson stood before us at the altar, he said, "Do you remember when, fifteen years ago, you committed to being together forever?" The day of our ceremony, August 5, 2017, would become a refresher class for us. It would be a day for us to really listen, remember, and at some point watch the video of our vow renewal ceremony and write down the points the pastor mentioned. We could use these key points every day as we continued to build a brighter future together.

Not only did my husband surprise me by getting the pastor who had married us fifteen years ago to perform the wedding vow renewal ceremony, but he also gifted me and our daughters with a picture-perfect lifestyle. He gifted us with a second home constructed from the foundation up that offers a lake view from our backyard, and he would later bless us with Drogo and Gi-gi, our English bulldogs. To top it off, we have the best neighbors we've ever had. We were actually able to build solid relationships with our neighbors, which would also contribute to our building a better relationship with each other.

Building a brighter future is also about being able to forgive others their transgressions. If you don't forgive others, you won't be happy within your marriage or within any of your relationships (those with neighbors, coworkers, family members, friends, and so on). Although I am talking primarily about my relationship with my husband, I can think of broken relationships that I've experienced with friends and family, and some that still remain unrepaired to this day. Some readers may have broken relationships with their children. Broken relationships involving anyone in your life can take a huge toll on your relationship with your significant other. When it comes to all relationships, the question continues to be this: Are you building a brighter future with this person, or has that ship already sailed?

You have to be strategic and intentional about having these relationship-building conversations. I have had these conversations with Jermaine multiple times, and I typically use a different strategy each time, one being to look extra cute on those days I plan to confront him. I have to lay the charm on thick. Building a brighter future also consists of what I mentioned in a prior section of this book, and that's sharing your vision of a successful relationship. Doing so gives a feeling of hope and confirmation that this is a meaningful relationship from which both parties can benefit. When it comes to my family and my husband, building a brighter future entails having family meetings, as successful marriages can be associated with successful businesses.

Finding time to laugh together is another ingredient to building a brighter future together. One of my favorite comedies is *Step Brothers*, starring Will Ferrell and John C. Reilly. This movie is a positive deposit into my emotional bank account because I am laughing all throughout the film. Other positive deposits are attending church and participating in family night. Having a date night and/or moment when we are laughing with our girls has contributed to the success of our marriage, and with the COVID-19 pandemic, we have found ways in which we can be even more creative in building a better future with our family.

CHAPTER THREE

The Journey of V: Valuing Family Traditions

A happy family is but an earlier heaven.
—George Bernard Shaw

Family traditions are very important. Traditions are unforgettable and precious moments that will strengthen your bonds with your significant other, your children, family members and friends. A family tradition can also bring people back together who have gone their separate ways. I've seen this happen firsthand. *Soul Food* is an excellent example of a movie that illustrates family tradition. It was the traditional Sunday dinners that brought family and friends together in this film. Family traditions can also bring together blended families.

In the next two moments, I will share with you some family traditions that are valued by my immediate family. My husband and daughters look forward to our annual Father's Day picnic and gathering together on birthdays and holidays. As a matter of fact, in January 2020 my husband and I had planned to be out of town for his birthday, but a series of events unfolded before the planned trip that allowed our family to get together on his birthday after all.

Moment Five: Father's Day Picnics

*Traditions touch us, they connect
us, and they expand us.*
—Rita Barreto Craig

The Burton family make it a point to gather together and enjoy each other's presence on holidays and birthdays. We play games, watch family movies selected by our children, sing along with karaoke, and devise creative activities to surprise each other. The Circle Boys Annual Father's Day Picnic is a tradition we created that would bring together not only our immediate family but our closet family members and friends as well. This day was designated as a day to celebrate the men in our lives. The Circle Boy family includes eight families: Mr. and Mrs. Jermaine Burton, Mr. and Mrs. Kevin McKinney,

Mr. and Mrs. Michael McKinney, Mr. and Mrs. Ahmand Smith, Mr. and Mrs. Darion Knight, Mr. and Mrs. Nicholas Sutton, Mr. and Mrs. Anthony Monegan, and Mr. and Mrs. Ronald Richards.

I woke up early in the morning on Father's Day ready to enjoy a day full of *fun* in the sun. The wives traditionally prepare for this day as we select the menu and choose the activities for the entire group. We have gotten to the point where we all wear the same color shirts, and we even take family pictures as well as the large group picture. I even purchased a big banner with pictures of the previous year displayed on it.

Every year in January, I pay to rent a nice location for our annual Father's Day picnic. This is for Jermaine. But what better way is there to collaborate and celebrate with people who share the same goal we do: to create and maintain everlasting marriages. One important point I want to make about collaboration is that you should make sure everyone in your circle (the other couples) respects your individual relationships and contributes a special part of themselves to this event. Our Father's Day picnics bring a circle of families together to eat, have fun, play games, and most importantly, build memories.

Moment Six: Gathering Together on Holidays and Birthdays

> *Tradition is not to preserve the ashes but to pass on the flame.*
> —Gustav Mahler

After embarking on the journey of learning how to be a mom, a wife, and trying to balance every other role that I play in my life—that of being a daughter, sister-in law, daughter-in-law, employee, boss, and friend, all of which I certainly have yet to master—it became time to start building memories with my husband and my four lovely daughters that would last a lifetime and be spread among the generations to come. Building traditions around holidays and birthdays is something that both my immediate and extended family will cherish and continue to participate in forever. It will ultimately result in them passing on these traditions within the families they build, and the traditions will blossom into stronger bonds being formed within their relationships.

Gathering together on holidays and birthdays is another tradition for our family. As a matter of fact, we don't just celebrate a "birth day," but we also celebrate birthday months! When it comes to holidays, if a friend or relative decides to host a holiday party on the actual day of the holiday (for example, December 25, Christmas), if attending would require the family to be separated, this is an event in which we would not participate.

The year 2020 is a year that would break the tradition of the Burton family gathering together on birthdays. This was a milestone birthday for my husband, and he wanted to go to Montego Bay, Jamaica, just he and I, and I was determined to make that happen. When you go to a place like Montego Bay and you stay at a Secrets Resort & Spa, taking the kids is not an option. So this would be the year the kids would not see us on the day of my husband's birthday, but would the universe allow this to happen?

I remember the tragedy like it was yesterday when we got the call that my husband's biological dad had passed away. The funeral was scheduled for the day of my husband's birthday in Fort Lauderdale, Florida, but we were due to arrive in Jamaica on that day. Without a thought, we scheduled a flight to Fort Lauderdale, and we pushed the Jamaica trip back in order to attend the funeral. As we packed our luggage and were still in the process of breaking the family tradition of celebrating his birthday with our daughters, we looked at each other and found comfort in the knowledge that we would at least be with our extended family in Florida.

As we approached the airport the day before my husband's birthday, it seemed as though we were going to be treated to a pleasant experience, but as the double doors opened to the airport and we walked in, we were immediately greeted by long lines all around the airport, snarling faces, and disappointing looks. As we went over to the baggage claim and entered our flight number, an error appeared. How did I forget the flight number? I searched through my smart phone and found the number, but it appeared to be the same number I had just entered into the system, so I tried entering it again. To my surprise, all flights were canceled because of the fog, and our flight was automatically rescheduled for the next day at 8:00 p.m. It was a nightmare. The funeral was in the a.m. part of the day, and we needed to get to Fort Lauderdale as soon as possible. My husband wanted to be supportive of his half sisters and brothers who were also going through a rough time dealing with the sudden death of their dad.

After standing in a long line for about an hour, we finally made it to the counter to speak with a clerk. "Are there any flights to any city in Florida tonight?" I asked the clerk. "We are trying to make it to a funeral." The clerk searched and searched and expressed to us that there was no flight to Florida that would get us to the funeral on time. My husband and I were in disbelief. We could not believe we would be missing the day we wanted to show our love and support to the Thompson family, but I sometimes ask myself, was this the universe allowing my immediate family to be together on his birthday? We rescheduled our flight to Jamaica for the day after my husband's birthday, so you know what that meant? It meant we would be spending his birthday with our four daughters.

We had nothing planned on the day of Jermaine's birthday because we were supposed to be at his biological dad's funeral, but because of the fog, we did not make it. We ended up not only spending his milestone birthday with our four daughters, but we all were together at House of Pizza catching up on life with the entire Burton clan: my mother-in-law Nikita, father-in-law Christopher, sister-in-law Christal, four daughters (Jada, Jasmyn, Jordyn, and Jade), and Jermaine. We were truly where we were supposed to be at that moment.

CHAPTER FOUR

The Journey of E: Enlarging the Family Vision

*I just want to thank God for
everything he has done in my life.*
—James Harden

I consider myself to be futuristic, and sharing my vision with my family is something that has brought us closer together. My vision poses hope, as well as gives us something to look forward to. It's also something that we think of during challenging times to keep us moving forward. Unlike many who have a vision board, I have a vision paper that I tape to the window in my kitchen with the hopes that God is looking down upon us and seeing the sparkle of my paper as the world goes round. My vision paper is made up of illustrations of goals and dreams that I'd like to see come to a reality. My vision paper incorporates the broad goals for my faith and family, health and wealth, and my overall plan of abundant living. The detailed steps that I will take to achieve those goals and dreams are in a little journal I keep near my bedside.

The saying, "The apple does not fall far from the tree," was proven when I found my oldest daughter Jada doing the same thing. She wrote her goals and dreams on paper and posted them on her window for God to see. Although I feel as though my story has already been written, it does not mean that my Heavenly Father would not spoil his daughter, because he has done so and continues to do so on a daily basis.

My husband and my daughters have our routine family meetings on Sundays, at which we share our individual dreams and aspirations. Not only do we talk about our goals and ambitions, but we also talk about how we will get there. One of my mentors, Joan Moore, has always been a believer of "plan your work and work your plan." So what did we do to plan our work and work our plan? In the next two moments, I will share how we began to enlarge our family vision together, and in my heart, this kept us all coming home with love.

Moment Seven: The Burton Billionaires

> *Vision without action is merely a dream. Action without vision just passes the time. Vision with action can change the world.*
> —Joel A. Barker

My husband and I and our children share so many ideas together. We share our goals with our children and each other, accepting that they may or may not be reached, but we know before we leave this earth, we are going to see one or many of those dreams come true.

To accomplish our goal of becoming the Burton Billionaires, we needed to set a strong foundation for our daughters. By scheduling and having family meetings, our daughters began to understand the power of organization and that generating a game plan for what they aspire to achieve is important. We are not a family who attends church every Sunday, but we are certainly a family who believes in God, and we believe there is power in the tongue. It has been said that "the family that prays together stays together." When we send up prayers, blessings will come pouring down, but we must get on our knees and pray as a family.

Vision without action will only result in a dream, and if you want that dream to come true, you have to be a doer and not just a talker. When we moved into our second home, I decided to take a dollar amount written on my vision paper and write the number on some sticky notes. I wrote "$50,000.00" on fifteen small, blue rectangular sticky notes, and then I posted the notes all around the house. I put one on the mirror at the entrance to the front door, one on the refrigerator, one on each mirror in all three bathrooms, some on the walls and in the closets. I did this when the girls were away from the house. When they arrived back home with their dad, I decided not to say anything. I would just document their reactions.

As I heard the car pull up, I got excited, knowing this would be an interesting moment. They opened the door and began to see the blue sticky notes. As usual, my husband didn't notice a thing. However, the girls were intrigued and wanted to know more. They began saying the dollar amount aloud—there is power in the tongue. They walked to the next room and read the number aloud again. As a matter of fact, they began doing something they'd never done before. They searched all around the house to see where and how many of these notes boasting "$50,000.00" they could find. The girls came back to me and said, "Mommy, is this a game, because we know how many stickies there are." They knew where each sticky note was, and they knew the specifics of how they were placed on the walls, windows, doors, mirrors, and in the closets. They'd begged and begged for me to tell them what the notes meant. I simply told them that this exercise was only meant to enlarge their vision, and I smiled and continued with my regular routine. After that moment, I kid you not, they started coming up with more creative ways of thinking. The girls even came up with their own game and other ideas for their lives. This was amazing to me. Now I know what your questions is, did the $50,000.00 dream come true? The answer is yes, that dream and goal for me in my lifetime has come true, and as a matter of fact, my cup runneth over.

Not everyone is interested in becoming a billionaire, and that's great. People's varied goals and dreams help to balance the world. Some people are already billionaires. Living an abundant life that balances spiritual beliefs, family, wealth, health, and education is an indication of a person who possesses true wealth. How would you rank the importance of the following in your life: money, friends, family, work, faith, and health? I continue to try to do a better job of balancing my life, but I don't always get it right. However, I have begun to focus on my strengths and managing my weaknesses. I have been rewired to understand that I don't have to be a well-rounded person to have an abundant life. All I need to do is be the star that only I can be, the star who collaborates with others who are the stars at what they do. We all need each other in this life. I learned this from one of my strengths' coaches, Beverly Griffith-Bryant.

Moment Eight: Showtime Exclusive Wheels

> *If you don't go after what you want, you'll never have it. If you don't ask, the answer is always no. If you don't step forward, you're always in the same place.*
> —idlehearts.com

The Burton family vision began to become a reality when my husband and I started our management company. However, his vision of starting his own YouTube channel about his wheels would be an action that would inspire us all. The "Show Squad," as he calls his viewers, should be ready for a show that is not only about his wheels but also about the discussions he has with his daughters.

My husband decided to create his first YouTube channel about cars. He was adamant about doing something new and doing something different for the new year. He was at a point in his life where he wanted to make sure he was able to leave memories for his daughters. Jermaine is the one who inspired me to begin writing this book to leave memories for our daughters. Creating a YouTube channel is an innovative way to create memories for your children and give them and other family members a place to go when they are thinking of you. The same goes for producing a podcast. It's just like having Facebook Live, and it's a cheaper version of Marvel Movies. Going back and watching Jermaine's videos is something that I do even now that he is still living, well, and with us. That fine, light-skinned man makes me laugh, and I get to see his potential whenever I look at his videos.

My husband began making his YouTube videos as a mini-sitcom. It is hilarious how he and Jasmyn banter back and forth in the videos about everything. Jasmyn was only fifteen years old at the time her dad began creating his channel, yet she was the editor and creator of the final versions of the videos. He gave her that ownership. They'd pull their joint vision together, and he and she would both make it happen. They would leave home and find the perfect spot to shoot the video. One very important part of this process was their customary stop at Dunkin' (formerly known as Dunkin' Donuts) to get a large Cappuccino Blast with butter pecan ice cream, caramel on the side (not in the cup), with caramel-flavored whipped cream and pecans on top. After my husband and Jasmyn (aka J-Camille) came home, it was work, work, work—time to edit the video and post it on YouTube.

At that particular moment, I know for a fact that enlarging our family vision was not my husband's sole intention. He was creating memories with our daughter while at the same time enlarging our family vision. The dream is about seeing and sharing the vision, creating a plan, and working that plan. You also have to commit to the plan regardless of whether or not it succeeds. Keep pushing because someone will like it. And if it gets in the hands of someone who can help sponsor your dream, the sky won't be the limit.

Parting Thoughts

Until we meet again, *Keep Him Coming Home* by learning about and loving each other, overcoming obstacles, valuing family traditions, and enlarging the family vision. Also, keep these learning points in mind:

Moment One: What I learned from this moment, "Driver's Education Class," is that it is important to reflect on the excitement you felt when you first met the person with whom you'd one day share your world. Try to remember the details of the meeting because you will need to recall these memories to motivate you when you begin to go through the stages of learning more about each other. In the beginning of a relationship, it's always good, but if you are in a relationship with someone for more than a year and responsibilities are attached to the relationship, circumstances will begin to get complicated and challenging. Why is that so? Well, how you got him is how you will keep him. I needed to make it a point to continue to be me on that first day and during that first month—me, Finesse, the girl who intrigued him and kept his attention. It is also important to be confident about what you do and how you move in the relationship so that you can continue to create that fantasy woman by being creative and strategic in how you handle situations. It is important to be who you are, an not compare yourself or your relationship to others. As for me, I may not be the sexiest woman, but I am sexy to my husband. I may not be the finest woman, but I am fine, sophisticated, and witty to my husband. I may not be the smartest woman, but I know what I have to offer. Most importantly, I know how to *Keep Him Coming Home with Love*.

Moment Two: What I learned from this moment, "Learning Our Strengths and Making the Relationship Work," is that if I am able to use my strengths most of the time within my relationships and manage my weaknesses, I can build a stronger bond with my man, my family, and my friends. If I can paint a picture of a successful relationship and gain buy-in from my man, this could lead to a strengthened and lengthened relationship which will *Keep Him Coming Home with Love.*

Moment Three: What I learned from this moment, "Reliving the Past," is that I have to be an active participant in my relationships, whether it's with my man, friend, or foe. Developing a bulletproof mindset when it comes to your marriage will help you to shut and lock the backdoor to the past, knowing that no one is perfect but also accepting that it is on you to work to keep your relationship sacred. Make sure to deposit positive thoughts, words, and emotions into your marriage to counterbalance the obstacles that will come your way. Continue to ask those important questions to move away from reliving the past, and focus on creating a brighter future. This will indeed *Keep Him Coming Home with Love.*

Moment Four: What I learned from this moment, "Building a Brighter Future," is that my past is my foundation, but it is not my today nor is it my future. Your past should serve only to make you stronger and more vulnerable to *Love.* The only way to build a brighter future is to move forward from the past and make the decision to focus on where you're going rather than on where you've been. There's nothing wrong with reflecting on the past, but continuing to relive past hurts can detract from the goal of building a stronger bond. Through my journey of growth and in revisiting the relationship goals I have written down, I have been able to identify ahead of time the obstacles that will hinder me and strategically build a game plan for success. Remaining positive and continuing to contribute to building a brighter future will without a doubt *Keep Him Coming Home with Love*.

Moment Five: What I learned from this moment, "Father's Day Picnics," is that it is very important to ensure that there is a day or a few days that my husband looks forward to, and being able to collaborate with couples who have the same goal in mind is always a great contribution to *Keep Him Coming Home with Love*.

Moment Six: What I learned from this moment, "Gathering Together on Holidays and Birthdays," is to cherish tradition and appreciate how valuable family traditions are. Our family traditions will keep us close during those challenging times and will ensure the building of a stronger bond. It has been said that life is short and we should cherish every moment, but because death is inevitable, we must also treasure the memories we've made and continue to keep the legacy of our traditions alive because, my friend, the worthiness of tradition will *Keep Him Coming Home with Love*.

Moment Seven: What I learned from this moment, "The Burton Billionaires," is that enlarging my family vision is really about living an abundant life, taking chances, trying new things (even though it may not make sense), and having fun. Our children will one day leave home and have to find their own way. The vision that my husband and I have instilled in them and the seeds that we have planted in them will help to keep them grounded and humble with the goal of living an abundant life. Enlarging the family vision will without a doubt *Keep Him Coming Home with Love*…all the time.

Moment Eight: What I learned from this moment, "Showtime Exclusive Wheels," is that building a solid and extraordinary relationship with my spouse is about our inspiring each other. That inspiration has kept us together for years, and it continues to keep us together. During those challenging times, we remember that we always have something to look forward to, something that we have been building together for two decades. You can be inspiring to people and not even know it. I also learned that if you go into something with a meaningful purpose and be intentional, enlarging the family vision will happen automatically, and it will *Keep Him Coming Home with Love.*

Coming Soon! Keep Him Coming Home with Love

"The Warmth of Your Home Determines the Temperature of Your Relationship."

Book No. II will focus on **LOVE:**

- **L**iving room decor
- **O**bserving serenity
- **V**iewing nature
- **E**ven tones with a splash of color

Acknowledgments

I'd like to thank my Father God, my husband of twenty years, Jermaine, and my daughters, Jada, Jasmyn, Jordyn, and Jade, as they are the inspiration for this book. Had it not been for your love and the memories we have created and shared, I would not have been able to write this book. I love you more than you know, and I will continue to protect you the best way that I can while I'm here and/or if I am away. I pray that you continue to keep coming home.

I'd also like to thank my team who supported and encouraged me to realize my goal to write and publish a book filled with valuable content in three months—a record time. My professional team includes my mother, Anniece Desceen Anderson-Owens, my brother and sister from another mother, Ankur Patel and Zarna Patel, my husband Jermaine, J-Camille Productions, S.H.E. Publishing, LLC, and Elite Authors.

To the people and entities who had no idea I was writing this book but were inspiring me along the way unknowingly. Those people and entities include New Smyrna Church of God in Christ lead by Pastor Jacob A. Pickett Jr. and First Lady Belinda Pickett, my dad Robert Hoskins, my stepfather Kenneth Owens and in-laws Mr. and Mrs. Christopher Burton, my best friend Sharaka Leonard, Ms. Diane Shula (former teacher at Overton Elementary School), Mr. Niznik (former teacher at Overton Elementary School), the Housewives of Rolling Meadows, Mr. and Mrs. Mondale Jamison, and Mr. and Mrs. Ahmand Smith (RB Pest Solutions). I love them all and wish them continued success in their marriages.

And to my Ace, I could not live life without you. My phenomenal mother helped me throughout this process, and she has been present in my journey and in every moment revealed in this book. My mother has always been my biggest supporter and is a powerful and transformational leader and mentor to me. She is my motivator, and she continues to inspire me every day of my life. I love you; later.

About the Author

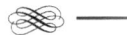

Born to parents Anniece Anderson-Owens and Robert Hoskins, Shenitha Finesse Anniece Burton grew up in Chicago, Illinois, in the Robert Taylor projects where she lived with her mom, aunties, uncles, and cousins. She attended Overton Elementary School, Marie Sklowdowska Curie High School, Pivot Point Hair School, Northwestern Business College where she majored in business, Purdue Calumet University where she majored in sociology with a criminal justice option, and Michigan State University in its nonbearing certificate program.

In Burton's lifetime, she has been employed at McDonald's as a cashier and fries cook, at Ford City Movie Theater in the concession stand, at UPS as a loader, and thereafter in the federal courts where she worked hard and was committed to delivering high-quality work, professional leadership, and creative solutions. Burton settled professionally when she was employed with the United States court where she was promoted through the ranks. Starting on the lowest rung of the ladder gave her an appreciation of hard work and dedication. She remains humble in all that she does, and she tries hard to put others before herself. Burton realizes that growing her leadership abilities and becoming aware of her signature themes have helped her to find passion in everything she does. She is a strengths champion who leads with developer, learner, input, futuristic, relator, achiever, self-assurance, responsibility, includer, and analytical capabilities.

Burton's hobbies consist of eating dessert before dinner, public speaking, writing nonfiction books, skating, playing the piano, reading, hanging out in the driveway or in the backyard with neighbors, and vacationing with her family. Burton is a life-long learner.